CONTENTS

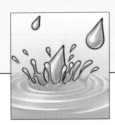

How do we use Water?

Water keeps us and all plants and animals alive. Our bodies will not work without it. We get water from our food and drink.

Water also keeps us clean. In a bath or under a shower, water washes away dirt and grease from our skin. We use water to wash our dishes, clothes, homes, cars and streets, too.

Clean water flows out of taps in our kitchens and bathrooms. To clean dishes, we add washing-up liquid to the water to remove fats and oils from the food.

Water

HODDER
Wayland

an imprint of Hodder Children's Books

Environment Starts Here!
Water

OTHER TITLES IN THE SERIES
Food · Transport · Recycling

Produced for Wayland Publishers Limited by
Lionheart Books
10, Chelmsford Square
London NW10 3AR
England

Designer: Ben White

Editor: Lionel Bender

Picture Research: Madeleine Samuel

Electronic make-up: Mike Pilley, Radius

Illustrated by Rudi Visi

First Published in Great Britain in 1998 by Wayland (Publishers) Ltd
Reprinted in 2001 by Hodder Wayland,
an imprint of Hodder Children's Books

British Library Cataloguing in Publication Data
Williams, Brenda
Water. - (Environment starts here! ; 2)
1. Water - Environmental aspects - Juvenile literature
I. Title
333.9'1

ISBN 0 7502 3485 7
Printed and bound in Hong Kong

Picture Acknowledgements
Pages 1, 4: Angela Hampton Family Life Pictures. 5: Wayland Picture Library. 6: Zefa Photo
Library. 8: Tony Stone Images/David Woodfall. 9: Tony Stone Images/Laurence Dutton.
10-11: Eye Ubiquitous/K. Wilton. 12: Eye Ubiquitous/John Dakers. 13: Tony Stone
Images/David Woodfall. 14: Eye Ubiquitous/J. B. Pickering. 15: Eye Ubiquitous/
L. Fordyce. 16: Zefa Photo Library/Norman. 18: Angela Hampton Family Life Pictures. 20:
Eye Ubiquitous/C. M. Leask. 20-21: Zefa Photo Library/Stockmarket. 22: Angela Hampton
Family Life Pictures. 24: Eye Ubiquitous/G. Daniels. 26: Frank Lane Picture Agency/David
Hosking. 26-27: Tony Stone Images/Vince Streano. 28: Angela Hampton Family Life
Pictures. 29: Tony Stone Images/Patrick Cocklin.   Cover: Zefa Photo Library/Stockmarket.

The photo on page 1 shows children splashing in water at the seaside.

We use water to clean our teeth and to rinse the toothpaste from our mouths.

Flowing Round the House

Clean water flows to our homes from pipes under the street. Pipes inside our homes carry the water to and from the kitchen, bathroom and boiler.

We each use about 30 bucketfuls of clean water a day. A toilet flush uses about 2 bucketfuls and a bath about 12 bucketfuls. The rest is water we use for drinking, cooking or washing dishes.

A plumber fixes a radiator to a central heating pipe. Hot water flowing through radiators heats air in rooms in the house.

Saving Water

Next time you take a bath, make a note of how far up the water comes. (Measure the height with a ruler.) Then, when you have a shower, leave the plug in and measure the height of water when you have finished. Which uses the most water: a bath or a shower?

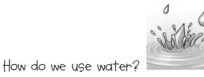

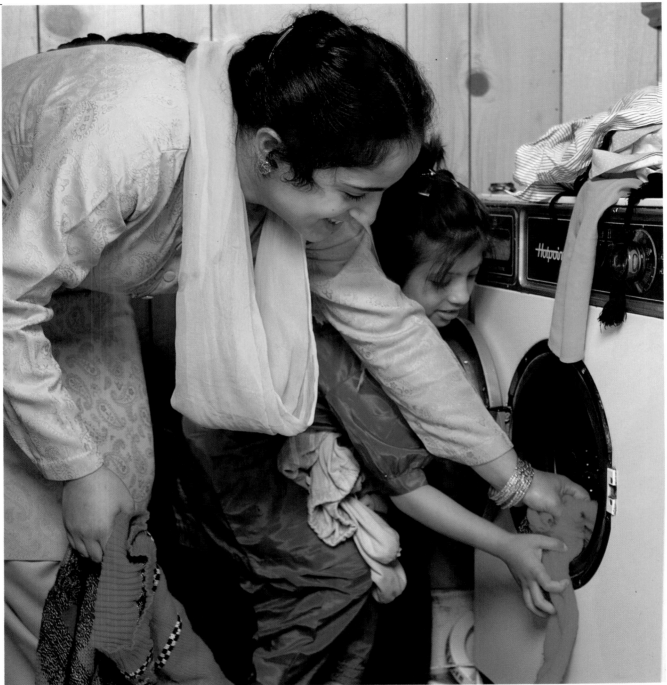

Water helps us all round the house. This girl and her Mum are unloading their washing machine, which uses piped water.

Where does the water go?

Used, dirty water with soap suds or bits of waste food runs away down a plughole. From here it flows down a waste pipe.

Water from a toilet carries away our body wastes. It flows down the waste pipe, too.

Dirty water flows from the waste pipe into a drain under the street. This runs into a bigger pipe called a sewer.

Flood water pours out of a sewer cover. When rainwater drains into sewers already full with water from houses, the sewers overflow.

Water flowing down a plughole swirls round in a spiral.

Down to the River

The main sewers are as big as railway tunnels. Waste water flows along them to a sewage plant. Here the dirty water is cleaned of all harmful germs.

At the sewage plant, muddy waste called 'sludge' is taken away and spread on unused land. Cleaned water then flows out into rivers and canals.

At a sewage plant, waste water from houses, schools, offices and factories trickles through filter beds that remove grit and harmful materials from the water.

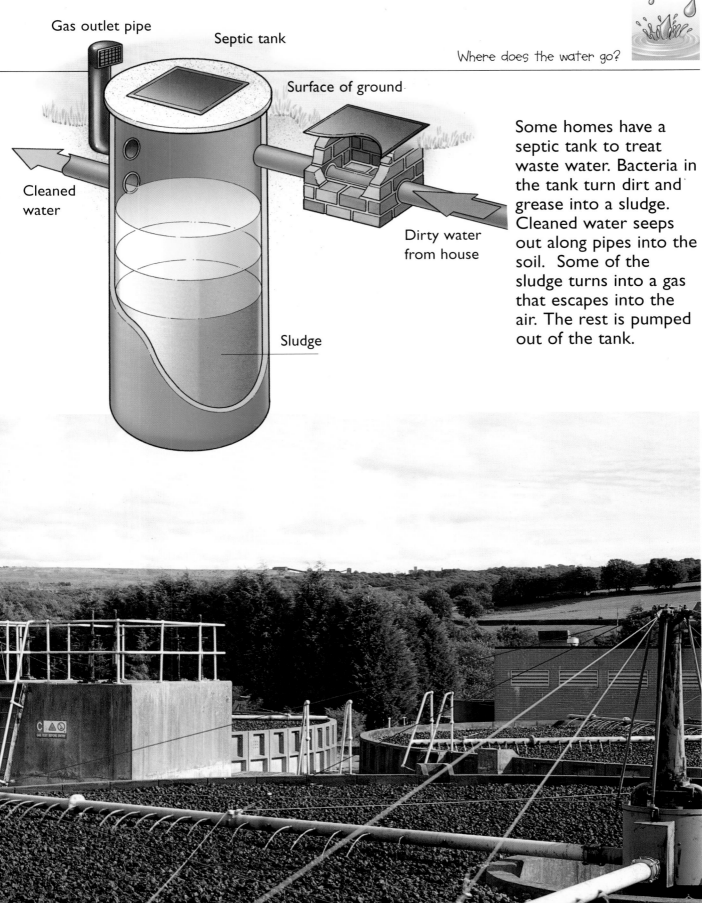

Gas outlet pipe

Septic tank

Surface of ground

Cleaned water

Dirty water from house

Sludge

Some homes have a septic tank to treat waste water. Bacteria in the tank turn dirt and grease into a sludge. Cleaned water seeps out along pipes into the soil. Some of the sludge turns into a gas that escapes into the air. The rest is pumped out of the tank.

Water in Seas and Sky

Rivers flow into the sea. They take with them water from sewage works and any factory wastes and rubbish thrown in rivers.

If too much waste material is dumped in the sea, it can poison, or pollute, the water. This may kill creatures living in the sea.

Sea water is too salty to drink. Here on the coast of Thailand salt for cooking is being collected from sea water.

Uncleaned sewage is sometimes pumped along huge outlet pipes like this one straight into the sea.

Steam rises into the air from huge chimneys at a power station. Steam is made when water becomes very hot.

Up into the Clouds

As the Sun warms the sea, some of its water turns into a vapour, or gas. This rises into the sky. High up, the vapour cools into water droplets that form clouds.

Smoke and fumes from fires and factories rise into the air, too. They mix with the clouds. Rain from these clouds may be so poisonous that it kills fish and plants.

Rain pours from thick, grey clouds that hang low in the sky.

To protect ourselves from the rain, we use umbrellas or wear raincoats. Here, sunlight has lit falling raindrops, making them easy to see.

Falling as Rain

Clouds are made of millions of water droplets. Tiny water droplets bump into each other and join to make bigger, heavier droplets. Eventually, the droplets become so heavy they fall out of the clouds as rain.

Rain often falls on high ground, then trickles into rivers. Rivers flow across the land and finally empty into the sea.

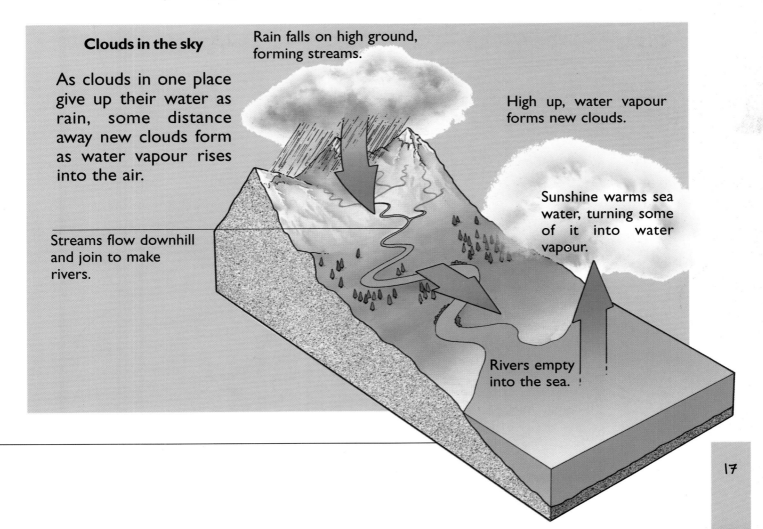

Clouds in the sky

As clouds in one place give up their water as rain, some distance away new clouds form as water vapour rises into the air.

Rain falls on high ground, forming streams.

High up, water vapour forms new clouds.

Streams flow downhill and join to make rivers.

Sunshine warms sea water, turning some of it into water vapour.

Rivers empty into the sea.

17

Water on the Ground

Next time it rains, watch where the water goes. It runs down drains in the road. It runs off roofs and soaks into the soil.

If rainwater cannot run away, it makes a puddle. Pools, ponds and lakes are like big puddles. They are hollows in the ground that do not empty of all their water.

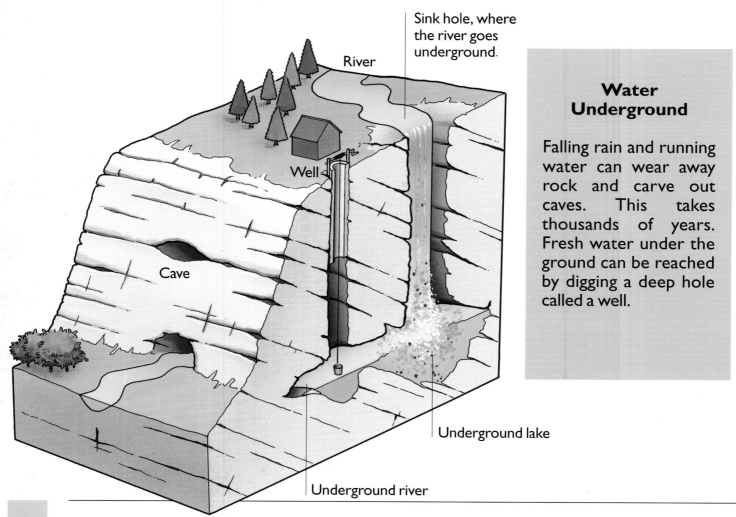

River

Sink hole, where the river goes underground.

Well

Cave

Underground lake

Underground river

Water Underground

Falling rain and running water can wear away rock and carve out caves. This takes thousands of years. Fresh water under the ground can be reached by digging a deep hole called a well.

Children swim in a pool filled by a river. The pool is a hollow in the ground at the bottom of a waterfall. It is known as a splash pool.

19

Frozen Solid

Snow forms when water droplets in clouds freeze into specks of ice. As the specks float in the clouds, they join up to make crystals. Then the crystals join to make snowflakes.

When the temperature is very low, water on the ground freezes. The water forms ice, which is solid and hard.

Near the North Pole, icebergs – blocks of ice bigger than a house – float in the cold waters of the Arctic Ocean.

In wintertime in some places, snow falling from clouds covers the landscape.

Water in Rivers

Snow and ice melt in warm sunlight. Melted water from snow-topped mountains rushes downhill into streams and rivers.

Rainwater collects in reservoirs and lakes. Lakes flow into rivers. Water for our homes is taken from reservoirs and rivers. But first the water is cleaned thoroughly.

Flowing water

Water flows with more force from taps in the ground-floor rooms of a house. This is because there is a greater weight of water above them, pushing down. To see this in action, make holes in a plastic bottle and fill it with water. The water flows with most force from the hole at the bottom.

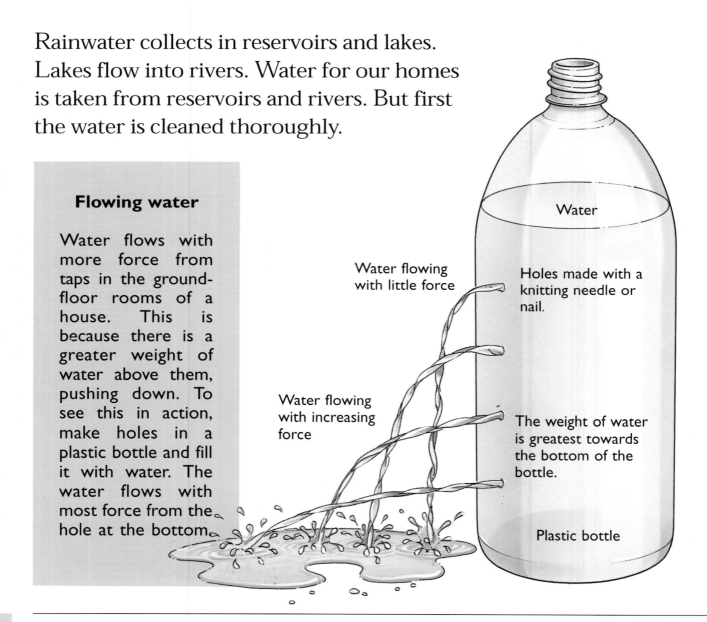

Water flowing with little force

Water flowing with increasing force

Water

Holes made with a knitting needle or nail.

The weight of water is greatest towards the bottom of the bottle.

Plastic bottle

Streams contain 'fresh water', so-called because it is newly made from rain. It contains little or no salt, unlike sea water.

At a water treatment plant, samples of water are taken regularly and tested to make sure the cleaning process is working properly.

Clean Water for All

River water must be cleaned before we drink it. Leaves, twigs, dead animals, plants, rubbish and sewage waste make river water dirty. Drinking it would make you ill.

River water is cleaned at a waterworks. Then it is pumped along big underground pipes called water mains. Small pipes take it from the mains to our homes.

At the waterworks

Fresh water from rivers is made suitable for us to drink or use in our homes at a waterworks. Some water companies add the chemical chlorine to fresh water to kill any germs. Often, they also add fluorine, a similar chemical that helps prevent tooth decay.

Water is stored, ready for use.

Water is collected behind a dam.

The filter beds trap sand, gravel and dirt.

Mains to homes.

A pumping station pours the water into filter beds.

Water from the dam flows into a reservoir.

25

The Water Cycle

The water we drink has been round the world millions of times. Each drop from your tap has been to a lake in Africa or an iceberg in the Arctic.

Drops of rain may fall on your roof, into the sea, or into the Zambezi River of Africa. Water moves from sky to land and land to sky, over and over again.

Water from Lake Victoria tumbles into the Zambezi River. The Zambezi flows into the Indian Ocean.

When heavy rain falls, a river can burst its banks and flood the surrounding countryside, as here in California, USA.

Saving Water

Sometimes there is not enough water to go round. In a dry summer, save water by not hosing the garden or washing the car.

Using Fresh Water

On average, we use about 200 litres of water a day. But we need only about 80 litres. One way of cutting down on the amount of water you use is to never leave taps running. Can you think of any others?

During a drought, when it has not rained for several weeks, it is best to water plants using a can instead of a hose.

To keep water clean and not block pipes, do not pour paints and oils into drains or allow sweet wrappers and pieces of paper to fall into sewers. That way, there will be clean water for the world's future generations.

Spring water (also known as mineral water) pouring into a glass filled with ice cubes. Spring water has little or no added chemicals like chlorine.

Water Topic Web

Maths

Measuring how we use water.
Learning about litres.
Keep records of daily recurring activities like "I drink water at...".
Keep records of dry and rainy days, for example "It rained on...".
24-hour timeline showing washing times, bathtimes.

Technology

Drawing a simple plan of house plumbing.
Making a simple water filter/fountain.

P.E./Dance Drama

Copying water animals' movements.
Rain dances.

Geography

The oceans.
Rivers and lakes.
How water affects climate and habitat.
Measure rainfall for a week.

Water

History

How did people get water before we had taps?
How did the Romans take a bath?

R.E.

Water in ritual, for example baptism, washing, bathing.
Water myths like the Flood.

Science

Plants need water to grow.
Pollution.
Water animals – ponds – oceans.
The water cycle.
Freezing and melting.
Evaporation and condensation.

Language

Sharing poems and stories.
Talking and writing about celebrations and festivals.
Phrases including water, rain, sea.

Music

Listening to Handel's *Water Music*, Tchaikovsky's *Swan Lake* and Mendelssohn's *Fingal's Cave*.
Singing nursery rhymes such as *Jack and Jill* and *Incy Wincy Spider*.

Glossary

Boiler A heater that burns coal, oil or gas or uses electricity to heat water in a building.

Chlorine A chemical added to water in swimming pools or at a waterworks to kill any germs.

Crystal A small solid shape with a regular pattern that some chemicals form when they change from a liquid to a solid form. Snowflakes, sugar and salt are made of crystals.

Cycle A continous round-and-round process.

Evaporation When liquid water is heated and becomes a gas called water vapour.

Filter Equipment that allows water to flow through but holds back sand, grit and other solids.

Ice Frozen water, formed when the temperature of the water falls below 0°C.

Plant Usually, a living thing such as a flower or tree. The word 'plant' can also mean a factory where goods are made or water cleaned.

Pollution Poisonous dirt, chemicals or artificial waste in air, soil or water.

Reservoir An artificial lake where water is stored for use by people.

Sewage Waste from toilets, baths and sinks.

Waste Rubbish, anything that is left over or not wanted.

Water vapour Tiny drops of water in the air; steam or clouds, for example.

Further Reading

Keeping Water Clean by Ewan McLeish (Wayland 1997).

Planet Earth by Lionel Bender (Kingfisher 1993).

The Water Cycle by David Smith (Wayland 1996).

Water by Kim Taylor (Belitha Press 1991).

Water at Work and *Water and Life* Science Starters (Watts Books 1994).

Water by Kay Davies and Wendy Oldfield (Wayland 1994).

What Makes It Rain? by Susan Mayes (Usborne 1990).

Index